MW01640292
Suitable for children aged 6-12
I'm As Good
As Everyone

Book Title: Encouraging Children's Growth Mindset

Author & Publisher: **QIAYI (INDIA) TRADING PRIVATE LIMITED**

1st Edition – 2021

ISBN: 978-0-578-32843-0

Printed By: **Fakhri Printing Works**
312/A Byculla Service Industries, D.K. Marg,
Byculla, Mumbai: 400 027, India.

Introduction

As children's main source of nutrition, books are of vital importance, which inspire their mind, cultivate their behavior, and develop their personalities. Thus, good books are indispensable for their growth and bright future.

As the first stage of one's life, childhood plays a significant role. A small habit in one's childhood, especially in the early stage, will have a great influence on one's character, sense of value, and even lifestyle in the future. With self-independence, self-control, strong heart, grateful mind, and confidence, one can embrace success.

Themes in these books are varied. What is more, two hundreds stories including fairy tales, life stories, and celebrity stories are involved. This set of books is more like an encyclopedia that can shape children's behavior and comfort their soul. Stories, knowledge, and mental exercise are available in this series, which is thought to be the guide that can help children overcome confusion.

Reading helps children to grow. Your child will be kindhearted, energetic, and positive after reading these books. Read them as early as possible!

Catalogue

Catalogue

Have Faith in Yourself

The Spring is like a gentle girl, she came quietly in a breeze.

Recently, shuttlecock became popular at Lily's neighborhood. Watching other kids playing shuttlecock while standing at the window, Lily wanted to join the kids. The colorful shuttlecocks jumped up as if they were beckoning to Lily. Lily couldn't resist the temptation of the shuttlecock. When she walked to the door quickly, Lily stopped in hesitation because she was afraid of not being able to play the shuttlecock well, thus being laughed at by other kids. When Lily's hesitant, her mother came by gently and picked up the shuttlecock. The mother patted Lily slightly on the shoulder and said softly, "Child, don't be afraid of failure, have confidence in yourself. Be brave

enough to try new things, and you may get unexpected results!"

Hearing her mother's words, Lily smiled and took over the shuttlecock. Just as she reached the playground, Lily stopped again. She thought to herself: mom sounds right, but what if other kids laugh at me? What if they don't play with me? How shameful would that be! Lily headed back as she thought of these. Then she remembered her mother's words. If one gave up before trying due to the fear of failure, then one would never learn. Even failure was another form of success, since

one could not success without failure. Hence, with all the courage she had, Lily walked to the other kids and asked, "Can I play with you?" Lily was grateful that the kids agreed. Out of her expectation, Lily played well at shuttlecocks!

When they were done playing, the sun shined upon Lily, as well as her heart. She was no longer confused, instead she was confident now!

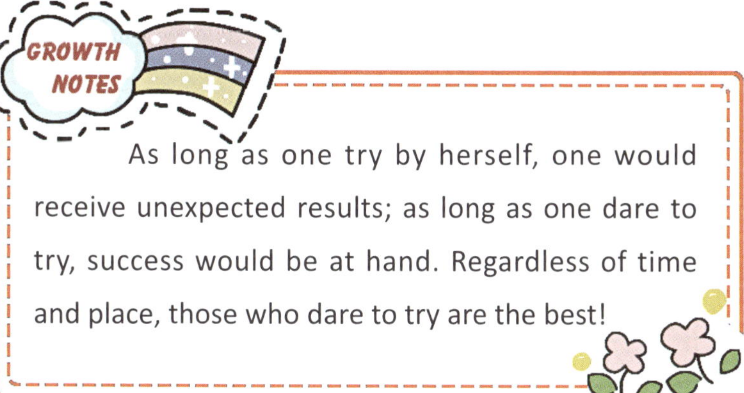

As long as one try by herself, one would receive unexpected results; as long as one dare to try, success would be at hand. Regardless of time and place, those who dare to try are the best!

Hang in There

Last March, George hurt one of his legs. After surgery in the hospital, he went through more than 4 months of treatment. The unbearable pain and the unforgettable hardship of rehabilitation treatment made George scream. He couldn't neither remember how he made it through or what was supporting him. Now what he could remember was one thing, that was after each treatment, he would tell himself, "Hang in there. You can do this."

When he went to school in a wheelchair, George felt mostly care from the class. What George didn't expect was, some students would mock him! And the humiliation even came from his former best friends before the surgery! It was clear to George that, those

students had no idea how ruthless and hurting their words would be. Neither would they know, nor would they understand George's pain during the treatment.

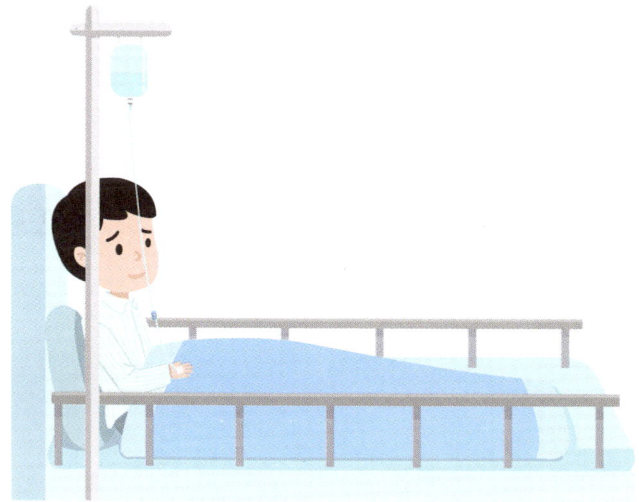

When George was fully recovered, his mother told him more than once, "You are the best. I'm not sure if I could make it through." Maybe it was only his parents that could understand George's feelings. He did not expect everyone to understand him. In fact, all he needed to know was: he did a great job. Since George made it through the most tough days of life.

Many people think that modesty is the only virtue, and self-apprise is a sign of pride. Though when we do something that are really impressive, it would also be encouraged to say, I'm the best!

The Birth of a Writer

Darkov is a shy boy, who lacks friend and self-confidence.

One day in October 1965, his secondary school female teacher Ruth Brazy laid a task in the class, asking students to read the article *"To Kill a Mocking Bird"*, and asked them to write a follow-up story.

Darkov wrote a follow-up and then handed it in.

Now he can't recall what the seventh place he wrote at the time, or how much the score given by the teacher Brazy teacher. But he still remembered that Brazy wrote four words in the blanks of his composition: "Writing is good", which he would never forgot.

These four words changed his life.

"Before reading these words, I don't know who

I am, I have no idea about my future," he said, "After reading her annotation, I returned home, I wrote a short story, this is what I have been dreaming. But I never believe that I can do."

In the remaining days in the middle of the year, he wrote many short novels, often brought them to the teacher. Brazy is constantly encouraged, meticulous, and amiable.

"She is what I need," Darkov said.

Soon, he was designated as the editor of secondary newspapers, responsible for the editorial work of the school, and was deeply loved by teachers and students.

His confidence has increased, and his vision has also expanded. Later, he was engaged in professional creation, writing a lot of popular work, and was praised by the readers, starting a more fulfilling,

harvest life. Darkov believes if there is no inspiring words on the edge of the composition, maybe today will be different.

GROWTH NOTES

In life, there are often big and small setbacks to hinder us. Sometimes we will stop being frustrated, caught in frustration and inferiority. At this time, if someone can give us encouragement, we will be confident and have the courage to defeat setbacks. Encouragement, can become the power of success; encouragement can inspire others; encouragement is a certainty of others. Encouragment is powerful, which contains care for others and makes people feel warm.

When others encounter difficulties and setbacks, we better encourage them to build up their confidence.

Learn To Be Confident

I was shy when I was a kid. I blushed when meeting a stranger, so not a lot of kids would play with me. When guests came to my house, grandma would usually introduce the cousins first, "This is Marble, she is very cute; that is Mark, he is smart; and..." then she pointed at me, "This is Marvin, he is... uh... good kid." I understood that grandma couldn't find anything to say about me, so she had to say that to comfort me.

This solitary mentality stayed with me until I went to middle school. Later I made it to the high school where everybody was somebody. In this group of overconfident kids, I have even low self-esteem.

Our math teacher, Mr. Goodman, was a serious-looking man, at his 40s. He was not approachable, but

very good at his teaching methods. It was said that his mathematics teaching was the best in town.

There was this exam, I had one mistake on my test paper. During the review I checked this question, and did it again. I found that my method of solving the question was actually better than Mr. Goodman's answer. It was much easier and direct.

So I went to him after class, claiming that my method was better. Or at least equally correct. So he should give me a better grade.

"Sir, I think I did right on this question," I said with few confidence. "Say again?" he asked, with his eyes

wide open. I repeated with a very low voice.

"Prove it, please." He stood up and hand me a piece of chalk, pointing at the blackboard.

I was so afraid to make yet another mistake, so I shook the head, grab the test paper and turned to leave. "Hold on, Marvin," Mr. Goodman stopped me, "If you believe you are right, you should be able to prove it."

"I figure it out already. You don't need to write it down." Mr. Goodman took my test paper and changed the grade. "I agree, yours is correct, and better. All you need is some courage."

Mr. Goodman's words inspired me. From that day on, I began to face anything and anyone with a straight attitude. Both in study and in life, I became more and more confident. My family and the class all see me grew like a cheerful guy.

Low self-esteem is often a personality defect developed since childhood. If it is not corrected at early age, it may affect a person's life. When you feel that you are inferior to others, it is likely that you establish a low self-esteem character. At this time, seek support from family, friends, teachers, classmates, etc., from the perspective of bystanders, they can help you break down low self-esteem and build self-confidence.

Life Is Not a Smooth Journey

One's life is not a smooth journey, and it is inevitable to suffer setbacks.

I was always interested in writing. I kept improving when I was a kid. Because of my good writing, I won awards and teachers' praise. So I was confident in writing.

Later I wrote and posted on my blog. In only a few days, I had thousands of views. I was thrilled in joy when looking at viewer's comments! Then, I kept post blogs every two or three days. My works had constantly attracted views, which made me very proud!

At the end of the sixth grade, I was going to take the middle school exam. I didn't have much time to write. Once the exam was over, the first thing I do was turn on the computer and checked the comments on my works.

My articles had only a few comments, while the essays of the literary club became very popular with increasing clicks. I was confused, thought for a while before I could find out the reason. Seeing other people's works so prosperous, I was at a loss, "Why others could get better review but me?" In addition, the article I newly wrote was not responded. I felt extremely uncomfortable. Just like a miner in a dark mine, I wanted to dig forward but in fear of the unknown danger ahead. Just as I was hesitating, a voice came, "Child, go ahead boldly!"

That was my dad, he saw me being upset, so

he came to help. "Child," he said, "life is not a smooth journey, it is often full of ups and downs, and any setbacks. You have to get up and keep trying. And remember that you are the best!" At that time I realized I was the best! After being hit, I cheered up and wrote again. Finally, I wrote an exquisite article with full intension. The viewership increased and members of literal club came to cheer for me.

After the setbacks, I learned how to deal with setbacks calmly, then headed step by step towards success. In this way, when I finally am successful, I can say loudly, "Actually, I am the best! I am really great!"

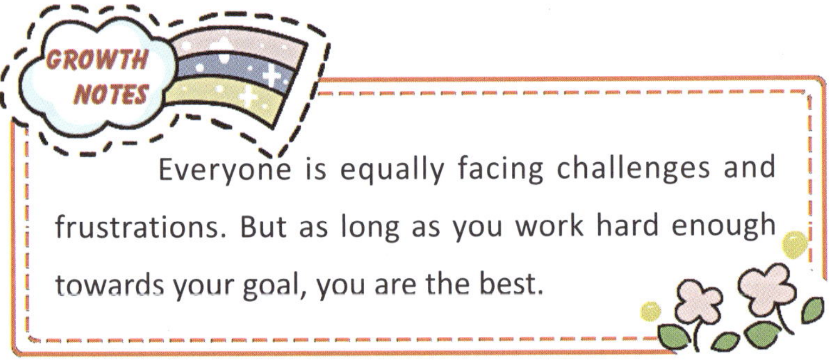

Everyone is equally facing challenges and frustrations. But as long as you work hard enough towards your goal, you are the best.

Andy Couldn't Fly

Andy was particularly good at drawing and riddling. Everyone said Andy was the best, and of course Andy believed them. "Who else is better than me?" Andy said to Moby triumphantly, "I can do everything!" "Can you fly high like a bird?" Moby asked, "Or floating in the sky like the clouds?" Andy thought for a while, "Yes! I'll make a pair of wings made of feathers, and then I can fly." As Andy said, he started picking up feathers.

Andy glued the colorful feathers together. With all the feathers he collected, Andy made a pair of wings! When the wings were ready, they looked so beautiful!

Bringing on his wings, Andy found Moby excitedly, "I have wings, I can fly now." "Really?" Moby touched his head in doubt. However, Moby still wanted to see what would happen. They came to a small grassy slope. Andy climbed up the small grassy slope, patted his wings like a bird, and then jumped hard. Andy was really flying!

But just when he was proud, something strange happened. Andy fell quickly like a rock...

Seeing that he was about to fall to the ground, a group of little birds flew by to help, and Andy landed safely. "Hey..." Andy sighed sadly while sitting on the ground. He really couldn't understand, "Everyone says I am the best, why can't I fly?" "Ah..." A sad sigh came from the tree, it turned out to be an eagle.

"Why are you sighing?"

"I lost my feathers and I can't fly anymore. How much I want to fly again!"

"Andy, come and think of a way to help him," Moby

said hopefully.

"I can't do anything, I can't help him." Andy was so frustrated, he didn't think he was the best anymore.

However, seeing the disappointed look of the eagle, Andy pitied him, thinking quietly in his mind... Finally, he thought of a good way. Andy found the remaining feathers and inserted them one by one on the eagle's wings. After a while, the eagle had another pair of beautiful wings. "I can fly!" said the eagle excitedly, "Andy, would you like to fly with me?"

"I... I can't fly..." Andy said embarrassedly.

"Would you like to sit on my back?" Eagle enthusiastically invited Andy. Now Andy and the eagle were flying together! They flew higher and higher... They flew into the clouds, and white clouds floated around them. Andy thought happily, "Although I can't fly, I can help the eagle. I'm really good!"

Do what you are good at well, you are great! Helping other children to complete one thing together is also great!

I Deserve the Praise

Once in a physical education class, the PE teacher assigned the task of five laps running. Five laps would be 1 kilometer! The students were a little unhappy. But I received special care from PE teacher, because of my poor health condition. All I needed was one lap.

When it began, I finished my one lap following other kids. While the others were still on the track, I was standing alone aside, looking very out of the place. So I told the teacher, I would like to do five laps as well.

Since I did one lap already, on the second lap, I slowed down. I was gassed out and worn out. On the third lap, I was soaked in sweat and began to walk. On the fourth, I was already exhausted. It felt like two iron shackles were tied to my legs. Even with all the strength

that I had left, I couldn't move them. I fell on the ground.

"Come on. You can do it." There was a voice in my head. Other kids were also cheering for me.

Right. I couldn't give in. I had to keep going till the end. So I tried my best to stand up, and did my fifth lap anyway. It turned out I could do something that I was not used to. I surpassed the old me, and that felt great!

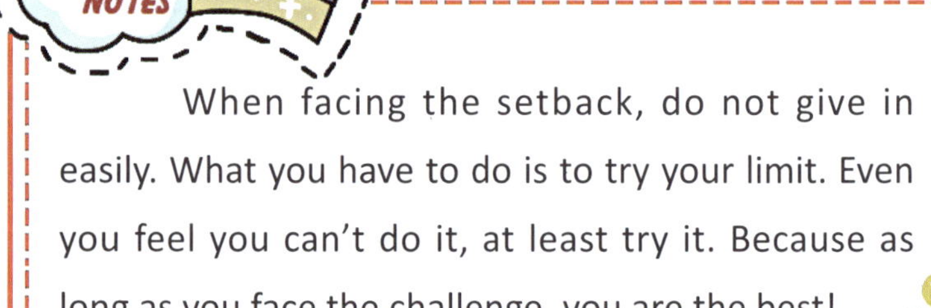

When facing the setback, do not give in easily. What you have to do is to try your limit. Even you feel you can't do it, at least try it. Because as long as you face the challenge, you are the best!

Baby Elephant's Nose

In the morning, the sun shined the entire woods, through the gaps of the leaves, the branches, and the mist.

To make the woods a better place, everyone worked hard. The woodpeckers were pecking. The monkeys were cleaning the branches. The squirrels planted the nuts in the groud.

Seeing that everyone had a job, the baby elephant sadly sat behind a tree. He was thinking, without a pecker, or the claws, or sharp teeth, he could do nothing helpful.

With that thought, the baby elephant cried.

Night came, the baby elephant was heading home, while he stumbled on the exposed roots. The baby

elephant became angry and picked up the root to throw it away, with his nose.

Suddenly he realized something. So he went home and told his mom that he found out he had a nose. Mom elephant laughed, said that the baby elephant had a nose since born. They both laughed together.

The second morning, the baby elephant woke up early. He picked up the branches to clean the ground, as he walk along the way. With him joining the force, it made other animals' work a lot easier.

Later on a small tree grew from the ground. Everyone were thanking the baby elephant's capable nose.

The baby elephant waved his nose proudly, thinking: why deny myself? I was actually great!

GROWTH NOTES

Everyone has his strength. The baby elephant finds confidence when he sees his strength. To get everyone's attention, and becomes one's true self, that is the meaning of life.

The Awesome Little Master

I was a fan of making aircraft model. I begged my mother to buy me a set of aircraft model. I would play with it sitting on the floor for hours, until my legs are numb. However, there were too many parts, and they were small. I often accidentally put the parts in the wrong parts, therefore had to start again.

After a few weeks, I finally assembled my PXT-22 fighter model! It looked cool! This week I just wanted to go back to my grandma's house. Of course I was happy to bring my model with me, so I can also show off. When I arrived, I first took out model and placed it on the table.

Oops! Accidentally, I dropped the plane model on the floor and broke it! The parts were scattered. My heart dropped together with the model. I cried as my

weeks of work disappeared. Just when I was discouraged, my mother came over and said to me, "As long as you have confidence, you can renew it! Crying can't solve the problem."

I listened to my mother's words, got courage, started to assemble it. This was my second assembled aircraft model. Because of the first experience, this time went much smoother. I was so focused that I forgot everything around. Practice did make me skillful. Then within only two hours, I reassembled the plane model! The PXT-22 fighter model also seemed to be smiling, "Little master, you are awesome!"

Looking at my beloved plane model, I am happy. Also I understand the truth of victory lies in persistence. I am really great!

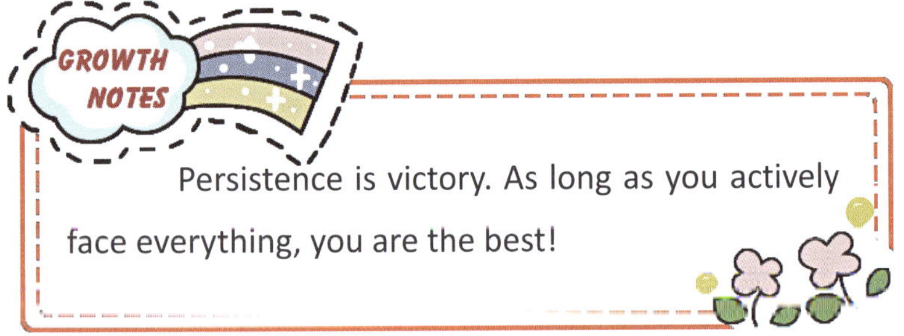

Persistence is victory. As long as you actively face everything, you are the best!

Little Squirrel's Red Coat

The little squirrel got up early. He washed his face and had a delicious breakfast. Then he was happily running in the house.

But after playing for a while, he suddenly found a lot of white things outside the window.

Wow! It turned out to be snowing. He looked outside of the window. The world is beautiful outside! Snowflakes were dancing in the sky. Then they slowly fail on the roof, pine on the ground, and earth.

The snowflakes were pushing the window and said, "It's beautiful in the world. With such a big snow, if you can pile a snowman, it will be fun."

The little squirrel decided to go and play outside. Just as he opened the door. He was blown by cold air, and returned.

Small squirrel stared through the window with an expecting look. How awesome would it be, if he could go out and play!

When his mother saw it, she gave him a thick and beautiful red jacket. Mom said, "Grandma made this new jacket for you. If you want to go out, put on this jacket, so you won't be cold."

The small squirrel happily put the jacket on, looked at himself in the mirror in front of the mirror, and ran out.

This jacket was really good. The fluff inside felt like a warm embrace of grandmother. Small squirrels did not feel cold any more. He went skiing, playing snowballs, and piled up a snowman in the snow.

Suddenly he saw a little monkey coming close step by step. The little monkey looked like he was almost frozen because of cold.

The little squirrel quickly took off his red jacket and then put it on the little monkey. The little monkey slowly warmed up.

The little squirrel decided to send the little monkey home. He shared the red jacket with the monkey, and walked to the little monkey's house. In their journey, they both felt the warmth from the red jacket.

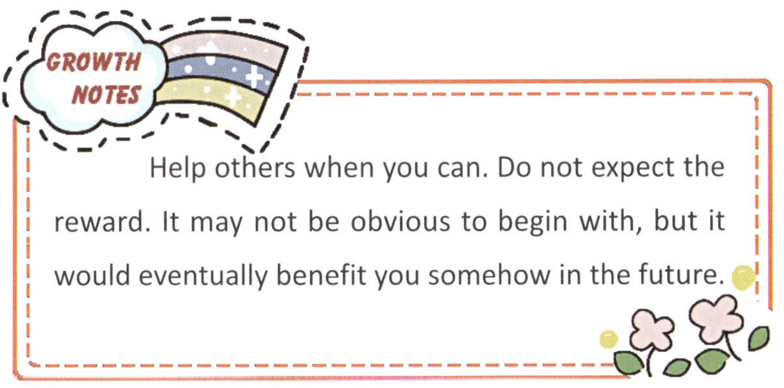

Help others when you can. Do not expect the reward. It may not be obvious to begin with, but it would eventually benefit you somehow in the future.

I'm Really Good

Penny was a competitor in the 800 meter race game.

Before the game, Penny heard that a strong competitor, Spots, who won the national championship, would join this game. Penny was very frustrated and worried about this competitor. Her coach came to comfort her, "Don't worry my child, you are the best." With the coach's words, Penny felt better.

The game started. Penny was at No. 4. She kept sprinting and made it to number 2, right after Spots.

The distance between them was only half a meter. At this time, Penny encouraged herself, "I can do it, I can do it." With all the strength she had, Penny speeded toward the end of the race.

Penny beat Spots and made it to the champion. The audience all started cheering for her. She felt that she was really good.

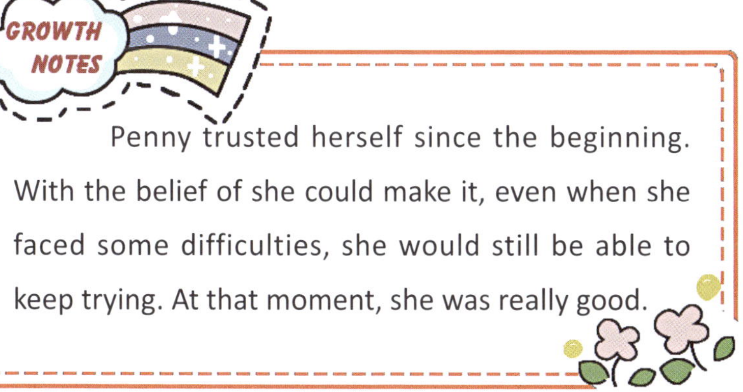

Penny trusted herself since the beginning. With the belief of she could make it, even when she faced some difficulties, she would still be able to keep trying. At that moment, she was really good.

The Piggy Moving Watermelon

The summer came. Watermelons grew big and juicy in the watermelon field.

The mommy pig took the baby pig to pick up some watermelons. The baby pig found the biggest watermelon and picked it up. He held the watermelon over his shoulder and tried to carry it home.

"Well it is heavy." The baby pig wiped the sweat from his forehead. Then he saw the little money were playing football at the foothill.

"I have an idea." The baby pig happily patted his head.

"The football is round, so is the watermelon. If the football can roll smoothly on the ground, so could the watermelon." The baby pig started to leave the

watermelon on the ground and started pushing it.

Mommy pig saw the baby pig was so smart to come up with this idea, she was so happy and praised baby pig. And the baby pig felt that he was so awesome!

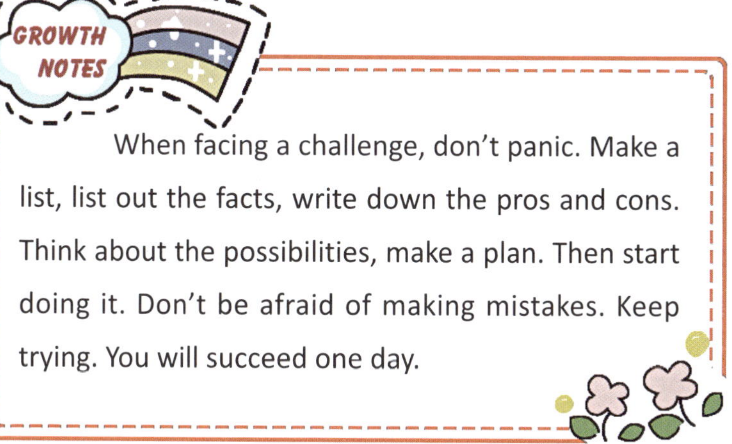

When facing a challenge, don't panic. Make a list, list out the facts, write down the pros and cons. Think about the possibilities, make a plan. Then start doing it. Don't be afraid of making mistakes. Keep trying. You will succeed one day.

The Little Rabbit With Low Self-esteem

The little rabbit was narcissistic. He often said it proudly, "I am beautiful. I run fast and jump high."

"What about me?" the little bird asked, "Don't you think that I am also very beautiful?"

"No!" The little rabbit said, "You can't run or jump as good as me."

"But I can fly," the little bird said, "and you cannot."

As she said, the little bird patted her wings, elegantly flew towards the sky.

"It's great!" the little rabbit was admired, "I also want to fly!"

So the little rabbit started to practice flying alone. But no matter how hard he tried, he couldn't fly.

Then he met the little lamb, who was making a

cake. "Can you fly?" asked the little rabbit.

"Of course not!" The lamb took out the cake from the oven, "I think I may vomit in the sky."

"What can you do?" the little rabbit asked.

"Many things!" the lamb replied, "I can make the best cake in the world."

"Maybe I should make a cake." the little rabbit thought after returning home. He mixed all the things he could find into the bowl, stirred for a while and threw the mix into the oven.

But after a long time, the smoke came out from the pot, and there was a very unpleasant taste.

"I can't even make a cake." The little rabbit felt very sad, so he ran to the old turtle.

"Can you teach me reading?" the little rabbit asked.

"Sure!" the old turtle said, "We start from knowing letters. This is letter A, this is the letter K, and this..."

The little rabbit opened the book and found that the book was filled with strange symbols. He did not recognize even one word. "This is too difficult. I am just a stupid bunny."

The little rabbit returned to the old turtle, depressed.

"I can't fly, can't bake, and can't read. I'm useless." the little rabbit cried.

"Neither can I! I can't fly. I can't bake. I can't run and jump like you!" the old turtle said, "However, I can read. Because I am an old turtle, and you are a little rabbit. It doesn't change the fact that we all love you."

The little rabbit went to the river to look at his own reflection. Suddenly, he realized his own strength. The little rabbit felt very happy.

The little rabbit should feel proud and be very satisfied with his specialties. But he found out things he couldn't do and started doubting himself. Everyone has his own strength. We should be proud of ourselves and never doubt ourselves.

Move Toward the Dream

In the graduation season, the literature teacher of the graduating class gave the students an essay titled "My Dream".

"Being a clerk in a big company!" "A scientist!" "A doctor!" The students had diversified answers. The teacher forgot the time and enthusiastically reviewed the student's composition. He found two essays special: one from David, a healthy kid with poor academic performance but a cheerful personality; the other one from Maple, a thin kid suffering from polio.

David wrote in his composition, "My father was originally a shoemaker, and he died when I was young. Therefore, I have no impression of my father. But I heard that my father is a skilled shoemaker, so I want to

become the best shoemaker." Maple's composition read, "My health is not good and I can't do normal people's job. Fortunately, I have a relative who works as a tailor. I'm not very skillful, but if I try, I will be able to make beautiful clothes. In the future, I have to become a first-class tailor." The teacher smile with admiration. It was like they planned together, David and Maple both wanted to be the best. These two humble teenagers had their own beautiful dreams and were full of confidence and hope for the future.

On the evening of the graduation ceremony, David and Maple went to the teacher's house.

"Sir, I decided to go to the shoe store as a trainee tomorrow," David said confidently.

"And I will take a three-hour train to the tailor shop. Soon, I will become a tailor." Maple's pale face was flushed.

"You both will head to the best in your business. This road will be full of hardships and difficulties, but no matter what happens, do not be discouraged." The two young men kept nodding their heads vigorously.

They didn't break their promise. Eight years later, they really became the first-class in their focus. David the shoemaker and Maple tailor were well known among the country.

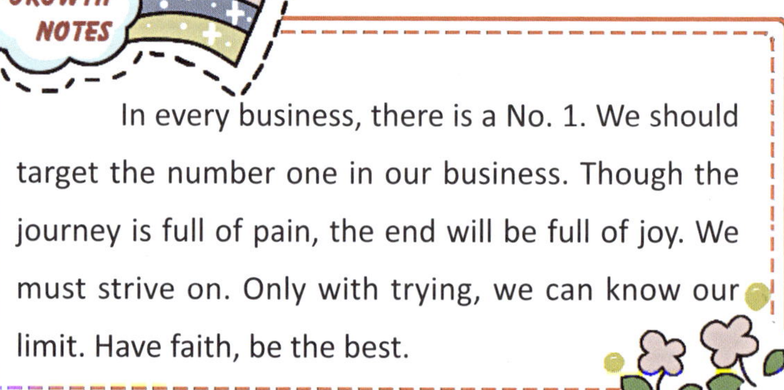

In every business, there is a No. 1. We should target the number one in our business. Though the journey is full of pain, the end will be full of joy. We must strive on. Only with trying, we can know our limit. Have faith, be the best.

The Coming of the Angel

Anna was born with a severe disease. After a serious of operations, she had two very obvious scars on her back. Because of this, she had very low self-esteem, especially in physical education, when other kids could happily take off their uniforms and put on casual sportswear, Anna always was hiding in the corner, secretly by herself. She had to put on sportswear fast, in the fear of being discovered by others. However, after a long time, other children still found the scars on her back.

"It's terrible!" "Monster!" as the hurtful words coming, Anna cried. After this incident, Anna's mother took her to the teacher.

Her mother told the teacher about Anna's birth. The teacher looked asked Anna with care, "Does it still hurt?"

Anna shook her head, "No. It rarely hurts now."

At this moment, the teacher had an idea. She touched Anna's head and said, "Tomorrow, please change cloth with other kids, I will be with you, ok?"

Anna was about to cry, "But, they will laugh at me again, call me a monster."

"Don't worry, I know what to do. No one will laugh at you. Really!"

Next day, in the physical education class, Anna hid in a corner timidly and took off her jacket. Right on cue, the kids came to mock her.

The teacher came in the room and walked towards Anna to check her back.

"These are angles' wings." The teacher looked at Anna's back intently. "I heard a legend. Some children are angels from the sky. And when angels become children, they take off their wings. Some little angels move slowly, and it is too late to take off their wings, therefore they have traces like this."

"Wow!" the children exclaimed, "These really are angel wings?"

"Yes," the teacher had a mysterious smile, "Do you want to check with each other? Does anyone has wings fallen off just like Anna?" All the children heard the teacher, and immediately checked each other's back.

"Ma'am, I have a little scar here. Am I an angle?" A child raised his hand excitedly.

"You are not. I have a red spot here. I am an angel!"

The children rushed to admit that they had scars on their backs, and completely forgot to make fun of Anna. Anna smiled with tears of joy.

The benevolent teacher used "angel wings" to free Anna from the weird gazes and walked out of the shadow of inferiority.

GROWTH NOTES

Sometimes unintentional words can hurt the caring person and make people feel inferior and introverted. We must not make fun of people that are different from ourselves. We must also correctly recognize our own difference and face it with a normal mentality.

Always Believe That You Are the Best

When a Wiseman knew that his time had come, he wanted to test and enlighten his best student. He summoned the students and said, "I don't have much candle left. I have to find another candle and pass on the fire. Do you understand what I mean?"

"Understand," the student said hastily, "your wisdom must be passed down very well..."

"But," the Wiseman said slowly, "I need the best inheritor. He must have considerable wisdom, he also must have sufficient confidence and extraordinary courage... Will you help me find one?"

"I will do my best." With the student's answer, the Wiseman smiled.

The loyal and diligent student began to look

around. He worked tirelessly through various channels. He brought in the candidates one after another, but they were all politely declined by the Wiseman. Once, when the student returned without success, the wise man said, "It's really hard for you, but the people you found are actually not as good as..."

"I must redouble the efforts," the student said eagerly, "Even if I have to search all over the world, I will have to find the best candidates."

The Wiseman smiled and stopped talking.

Half a year later, the wise man was about to succumb to the world, and the best candidate still was

nowhere to find. The student returned ashamed, "I'm so sorry, I disappointed you!"

"I'm not disappointed, but I feel sorry for you." The Wiseman closed his eyes and paused for a long time before he said bitterly, "Originally, the best candidate is yourself, but you failed to believe yourself. In fact, everyone is his best. One just has to discover, know, and value oneself..."

The students regretted it very much and even blamed himself for the rest of his life.

To not regret like that student, everyone who yearns for success should remember this: Always believe that you are the best!

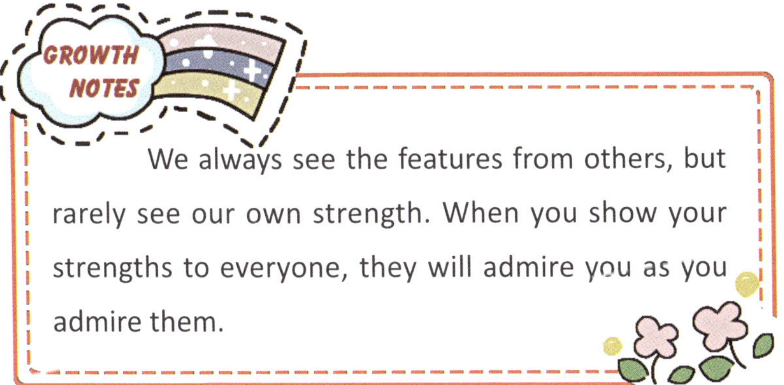

We always see the features from others, but rarely see our own strength. When you show your strengths to everyone, they will admire you as you admire them.

The Teacher With Magical Power

In a small village called Hogg in a poor area, there was only one elementary school with one class for each grade. However, it was said that one teacher possessed magical power. Almost every year, several students were accepted by universities, which made Hogg Village reputable. Now that all the folks from nearby villages, did everything possible to send their children here.

The legend of magic started four decades ago, when a 51-year-old college professor transferred to Hogg village primary school. The headmaster of the village claimed this teacher had great knowledge, so he would always be right.

None of them saw a university professor before. So hearing the village headmaster, they all felt even more

amazing. Therefore, children and adults all admired the old teacher as a god, and believed in whatever he said. After teaching for some time, the old teachers found out the students naughty, rebellious, and had no interest in learning. This gave him quite a headache.

Not long after his found, a shocking news came out from the village. It was said that the old teacher could use magical power to tell a child's fortune. The reason was that, children went home and told their parents, the teacher foretold one could become a mathematician, the other a writer, and the third a musician.

Soon, the parents discovered that their children were not much the same as before. They became sensible and interested in learning, as if they were really mathematicians, writers, and musicians. The mathematician-to-be started learning mathematics harder; the writer kid had outstanding literature performance. The children shifted their desire of playing to study. Even without strictly discipline, the children would study by themselves. They all had the belief that they would all be excellent in the future, and they knew bad habits would not help them.

A few years after, a miracle happened, most of them were admitted to the university with excellent results.

When the old teacher retired, he had to return to the city. He passed on the magic to the new teacher. And the new teacher kept foretelling young student's fortune. They all kept a secret of the magical power from the villagers.

As to the college graduate from Hogg village, they

had realized this secret from the moment they were admitted to college. But they all consciously kept this secret. That respectable old teacher did not have real magic, but sow faith in these young children's mind!

GROWTH NOTES

Just like there is no magic spells in this world, a person's fate is not already destined. The sheer reason these children can achieve impressive results, is because they are full of confidence, and hard work. As long as one is willing to believe in himself, and keeps trying toward the goal, one can become the kind of person he wants to be.

Make Weakness Our Strengths

John loved ballet as he grew up practicing it. Unfortunately, in a dance training, he had a neck injury, after which his neck was like a crooked poplar tree. His friends all felt sorry for him, as his ballet life was gone. A few years later, in the class reunion, everyone was surprised to find that John had become a top violinist in a famous orchestra. With a violin on his shoulder, his crooked neck posture was no longer a flaw. His posture became a beautiful spiritual shock. When asked about the secret of his success, John said that because of his neck injury, he did not feel uncomfortable when practicing violin. He felt that this posture was just right for him, and he practiced violin for longer and harder than anyone. Over time, he became the backbone of the

orchestra.

Once there was a farmer in California, who spent a lot of money to purchase a land. Yet it was barren land that wouldn't grow any crop. The farmer was frustrating. One day, he found that actually a lot of rattlesnakes were hidden within the bushes. With an idea, he decided to breed rattlesnakes in large numbers on this terrible land. Later, he turned his farm into a tourist site exclusively for exploration and sightseeing. Tourists were attracted from all over the world. It wasn't the land that changed, but the farmer himself.

Maybe you have complained about such defects in yourself. But with the positive and enterprising mentality, and can enjoy the misfortune as a gift, we can find success from our defects. Hence I believe you can do it.

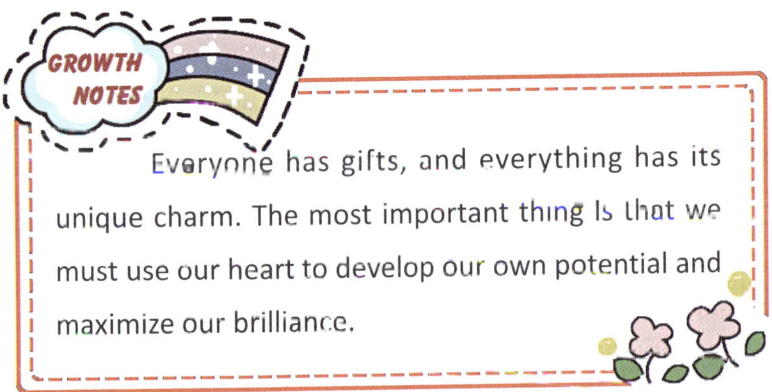

Everyone has gifts, and everything has its unique charm. The most important thing is that we must use our heart to develop our own potential and maximize our brilliance.

The Confident Painter

A young painter drew a picture and planned to sell it on the street. When a rich man favored the picture and asked how much it was, the young artist did not hesitate to quote 500 US dollars. The rich man felt it was a bit expensive, so he asked for a lower price. The young painter refused to offer a lower price, as he tore the painting into pieces.

The rich man was very surprised, "Young man, why tear it up? What a pity! If you can't sell it for $500, you can always ask for less! Are you mad at something?"

"Sir, I'm not mad at anything. I asked for $500, because I think this painting worth the price. The fact of you bargaining with me, shows that it is not good enough and not worth the price. So I will continue to practice and

try better next time, until the customer admits it." the young painter said calmly.

This young painter did not want to be conceited and believed that his painting worth 500 dollars. With his diligence, he eventually became a master painter of the generation. He left behind many masterpieces, which all worth a lot more than 500 dollars!

When selling that painting, the young painter was lived in extreme poverty without fame. Although he needed money, he still wouldn't under sale himself. It was this confidence and courage of not despising himself that made his success.

GROWTH NOTES

No matter what the challenge is, we should never underestimate ourselves. With the confidence and courage, we can make ourselves better and recognizable.

The Secret of Success Is to Believe in Yourself

Abraham Lincoln was the 16th President of the United States. Thirty years before he became the president, no one thought this poor boy could later become one of the greatest presidents in American history.

He didn't born a good looking child. His voice was hoarse as he stammered, and he was always slower than other kids. For this reason, the kids he grown up with often made fun of him.

He had a very miserable childhood compare with his peers. He was born in a poor family where his father was a shoemaker. He could barely get enough food and clothing. He lost his mother at the age of 9 and received only 18 months of non-formal education. Sometimes,

even for the simplest math calculation, it would take him half an hour to work it out. And he always messed up even the easiest thing. Fortunately, the stepmother treated him as her own. She never scolded him, instead she encouraged him, "At any time, don't care what others think of you, you just need to believe in yourself, and you will do it."

After he grew up, young Abraham became a ferryman on the Ohio River, to make a living. He then became a plantation worker, a stonemason, a shop assistant, and a carpenter. He was fired by his employer 11 times.

In 1836, Abraham became a lawyer through his own hard work. During this period, he learned deeply about the misery of the American people at the bottom of society. He realized that in order to save the people from the dire straits, political means must be taken. Since then, he decided to become a politician. In the next 20 years, he was repeatedly elected congressman, but he failed 8 times for presidency.

In 1856, he fought for the nomination of vice president at the Republican National Convention. He won less than 100 votes and once again failed miserably.

During a presidential debate, a reporter asked a tricky question to Abraham and his competitor, "Now if you two vote for the president, who would you vote?" The competitor shrugged and replied calmly, "I refuse to answer this question. It should be the great people to decide who shall be president." But Abraham took a big step forward bravely and said loudly, "I will vote myself. Because only I am the most suitable leader for you." There was thunderous applause from the audience.

GROWTH NOTES

We cannot choose our origin, but we can decide our future. No matter what environment, no matter how others think of us, we should believe in ourselves and move toward our goals. One day we will make our dreams true.